HANDBOOK
FOR
DEACONS

by
Dr. J. D. O'Donnell

Randall House Publications
114 Bush Road P.O. Box 17306
Nashville, Tennessee 37217
Roger C. Reeds
General Director
1973,

Dedicated to
my father,
Alfred O'Donnell
and
my grandfather,
Daniel O'Donnell
Both deacons

PREFACE

I have the highest respect for the office of the deacon. Raised in a deacon's home, I heard the Word of God read every night and gathered with the family in a prayer circle while my father prayed. When I spent the night at my grandfather's house, the same procedure was followed. My grandfather was a deacon too. These two men instilled in my heart a love for the Word of God and a dedication to the work of Christ. Their example in life was an inspiration to me.

As a pastor, I have many pleasant experiences to remember with deacons. In my first church I had only one deacon. He later, like Stephen and Philip, became a preacher. I remember other deacons who have shared with me in the times that I was sacrificing and struggling to stay in the ministry on a full-time basis. I'm sure that every preacher remembers such men in their lives with great thankfulness.

This book is written with the desire that it will challenge all of our deacons to a greater scope of service. If its standards seem high, let it be remembered that the character of Christ is to be the goal of us all. His example is our pattern in all things. Falling short of this, we must ever be reaching forth for higher attainments in His service.

J. D. O'Donnell
January 1973
Springfield, Missouri

CONTENTS

CHAPTER 1
Origin of the Office 8
CHAPTER 2
Qualifications of Deacons 20
CHAPTER 3
Selection of Deacons 32
CHAPTER 4
The Service of Ordination 44
CHAPTER 5
A Deacon's Relationships 52
CHAPTER 6
Organization of the Board 62
CHAPTER 7
Responsibilities and Duties 72
CHAPTER 8
The Spiritual Welfare of Members 82
CHAPTER 9
Missions and Evangelism 92
CHAPTER 10
Stewardship and Church Finance 98

Chapter One

ORIGIN OF THE OFFICE

A. The Widows' Emergency
B. The New Testament Development
C. The Deacon In History
D. Reasons For Deacons Today

Chapter One

ORIGIN OF THE OFFICE

The distinct origin of the office of the deacon has been lost in antiquity. There is no event to which one can point distinctly and say that it is the first election of deacons.

A. The Widows' Emergency

The story in Acts 6:1-8 is generally alluded to as the first election of deacons. Indeed it must be looked upon as the origin of the office even though the men were not called deacons nor conceived to be such at this time.

The seven men in Acts 6 were selected to perform a certain specific mechanical or secondary task. This task had to do with the distribution of material benefits to fill the needs of the widows in the Jerusalem church. The apostles were becoming weighed down with these secondary tasks and felt that more important functions demanded their attention. Therefore, seven men were chosen to minister to the needs of the widows while the apostles gave themselves "continually to prayer, and to the ministry of the word" (verse 4).

It is true that the inspired record gives very vivid details of a larger ministry performed by some from among these seven, but there is no passage of the

Scriptures which suggests that those activities were related to or resulted from their appointment as one of the seven. Their specific appointment as one of these seven men was to distribute relief to the widows in need.

The work of Stephen, mentioned in Acts 6:8 ff., is entirely beyond the scope of the appointment he received in verses 1-3. The same may be said of the activity of Philip (Acts 7:5-40). His evangelistic work was over and beyond his appointment as one of "the seven."

The election of the seven men in Acts 6 was probably the forerunner of the office of deacon. These men were chosen to perform a special task—to care for the widows. As the term, deacon, came to be used in the New Testament, it refers to men who were chosen to a particular task in the church. The Greek word for "deacon" describes the work of a servant. It seems that the young church saw a need for an officer or officers in the church to be designated for specific services. These services relieved the ministers for the preaching of the Word and evangelism. Thus, within a brief period two distinct offices arose in the church. The elder or bishop was comparable to the pastor in today's church; the deacon was the other.

B. The New Testament Development

There were more words than one in the Greek to describe a servant. Paul used one word to describe himself as a servant of the Lord (Romans 1:1; Philippians 1:1). That word refers to one who gives himself in a permanent relation to do the will of another. The word for "deacon" also referred to a servant or to one who "executes the commands of another." It refers in John 2:5, 9 to waiters or people serving food and drink. In Matthew 22:13 this same word is used to describe servants (deacons) who served a king and carried out his orders. The same word is translated "minister" as Jesus used it to describe one who serves another (Matthew 20:26) or as one in the lowliest position (Mark 9:35). Even earthly governors through whom God carries out His administration in the earth are designated by this term.

At the first, this word had a general use in the church to describe anyone who ministered in any particular task in the church. Paul describes himself as a deacon or servant *(minister,* in the King James Version) as he promoted the work of Christ (Colossians 1:25). He referred to himself and Apollos by this same designation in 1 Corinthians 3:5, and broadened it to cover many more in 2 Corinthians 6:4. In one of his earliest epistles he referred to Timothy as a deacon or servant (1 Thessalonians 3:2).

From this general use, however, the term was soon to take on a particular meaning in the church. It came to refer to a particular office. In fact, it seems already to have taken on this particular meaning when Paul wrote to the Philippians (1:1) for he mentions the two offices (bishops and deacons) which came to be used in the early church. Bishops (synonymous with elders) were in the church almost from the beginning (Acts 11:30). Even on the first missionary journey Paul ordained elders in the newly constituted churches. The mention in Philippians 1:1 is the first one which definitely refers to the office of a deacon in the church. The only exception might be the reference to Phebe as a servant (or deaconness) from Cenchrea (Romans 16:1). This woman was one assigned to a particular task rather than to an office.

The Book of Philippians was written while Paul was in jail in Rome during his first imprisonment (around A.D. 61). He was in the Roman jail and was aware of such an office in the church at Philippi, therefore it can be assumed that the office had been in existence for some time.

It was not until Paul's release from imprisonment in Rome that the most specific reference is made to the office of the deacon in one of his epistles (1 Timothy 3:8, 10, 12, 13). By this time (around A.D. 65) the office was a common one in the churches and Paul gave specific directions regarding these officers to Timothy in

Ephesus (1 Timothy 3). The distinction in the office of pastor ("if any man speak") and deacon ("if any man minister") might have been intended by Peter in his epistle of about the same date (1 Peter 4:11). The word "minister" in this Petrine passage comes from the same root word as *deacon* and refers to the act of serving.

C. The Deacon in History

With the passing of time, more specific directions regarding the responsibilities of various officers in the church developed. The church grew and so did the number of officers in the church. In fact, by the end of the first century, three offices are mentioned in the writings of the church fathers. The office of bishop and elder had become distinguished as two orders of clerics, and the deacons were a third order and lowest in rank. With this departure from the New Testament pattern, the idea of the distinction between the cleric and the laity also grew. This concept in time was to bring evil results upon the church. As the orders developed and as these clerics became distinguished from the laity, a strong hierarchical framework developed in the church. The clergy came to dominate the church. Bishops over the churches of a large city grew in power. The next step was bishops over areas of the country. The ultimate development was the pope over the whole church, bishops over sees, priests over churches, and the deacon played a very minor role in the worship.

When the Reformation came, the renewed concepts and ideas regarding the deacon varied from group to group. In the Roman Catholic system the deacon is an assistant at the altar. He is counted a member of the priesthood. He is also a member of the priesthood in the Church of England. He performs certain ritualistic tasks as reading the Scriptures and assisting the priest. However, he does not have the authority to consecrate the sacramental elements. Neither can he pronounce absolution.

In a congregational type of church, the movement has been toward a restoration of the New Testament concept of the deacon. Neither the deacon nor pastor has ecclesiastical authority. The effort is always to teach the concept of the priesthood of all believers. The authority of either pastor or deacon is personal and not ecclesiastical. A deacon's authority in the church is determined by the influence of his personal character and Christian testimony. Just as the pastor, so the deacon is a personal leader at work for the Lord. It is through the lowliness of service that the deacon is to rise to influence the church. He is faithfully to perform the task given to him by the church and humbly serve in the capacity to which he has been elected.

D. Reasons for Deacons Today

The reasons for the office of deacon remain primarily the same as that found in the New Testament. Of course, the chief reason for the office is found in the fact that it is one of the two offices found in the church of New Testament times. The Scriptures are the basis upon which a local church should be formed and the means through which it is to be built up in the Holy Spirit. The authority of the Scriptures needs to be recognized and upheld in a marked manner by all who compose the church. Common sense is good and has led to many important aspects of Christian service and work. However, no organization which has not followed the general trend of scriptural teaching has added to the efficiency of the work of the Lord. The basic and simple organization as revealed in the New Testament has always produced the most effective witness for Christ. The divine origin of this office gives it significance and eternal usefulness.

The office of deacon was set up to free the pastors for more pressing tasks. Just as Moses organized a group of leaders to free him from the details of his work and to allow him more strength for vital duties, so the Holy Spirit led the apostles in granting officers to the church who would free the pastors for the chief tasks. This principle was present in the choice of the seven (Acts 6) and certainly was in mind when Paul described deacons to Timothy (1 Timothy 3).

The office of deacon was instituted to release the pastor in the church when its organization was very simple. In the more complex organization of today, the deacon is more greatly needed than ever before. In a large church the administration of the staff alone could consume all the pastor's time. Shut-in and hospital visitation could be another full-time ministry. Deacons can be used to relieve pastors from so many of these extra duties so that he can have proper time for prayer, meditation, the reading of the Bible, and sermon preparation.

Deacons are needed to give the church a more effective witness. After "the seven" were elected, the Book of Acts reports that "the word of God increased; and the number of disciples multiplied in Jerusalem greatly" (6:7). At any time the witness of the pastor is supplemented through the witness of laymen, the effectiveness of the witness is multiplied manifold. Even if the work of the deacons only frees the pastor for greater witness, the effect can be great. But it is much greater when the deacons begin witnessing after the example of Stephen and Philip.

Deacons should be an effective force for dynamic leadership in the church. The power of his leadership was never intended to be a force to attain his own ambitions in the church. Rather he is to coordinate the force of his leadership with that of the pastor. His influence should support the pastor who is the elected leader of the church.

In his position as a leader in the church, the deacon can promote the harmony of the church. The seven chosen men in Acts 6 healed a breach in the church fellowship and restored harmony to the church. Factions are often promoted by deacons rather than healed by them. No deacon should ever be guilty of this. As a layman he can often feel the pulse of the people in ways that the pastor cannot. When he is aware of dissension or any dissatisfaction among the members, the deacon should labor to resolve the problem. If there is any murmuring against the pastor, he should work to maintain the respect of the members for the pastor's leadership. He has no right to promote disharmony in the church.

There are many needs of church members that can be filled by a deacon. As he undergirds the work of the pastor, he can often give quiet counsel to a member. Many times there are small needs within the congregation that might escape the notice of the pastor. Some can be handled by the deacons. Others need to be called to the attention of the pastor.

Thus, the office of deacon was established as a supporting ministry to the pastor. This office, born under divine direction, can be a vital force for leadership in our churches and an important means of advancement of the Kingdom of God. "Covet earnestly the best gifts," Paul admonished (1 Corinthians 12:31). The call to the office of a deacon is surely one of the best gifts.

Chapter Two

QUALIFICATIONS OF DEACONS

A. Essential Characteristics
  1. Of Honest Report
  2. Full Of The Holy Ghost
  3. Full Of Wisdom
  4. Full Of Faith

B. Biblical Qualifications
  1. Grave
  2. Not Doubletongued
  3. Not Given To Much Wine
  4. Not Greedy Of Filthy Lucre
  5. A Strong Spiritual Life
  6. Proved
  7. Good Domestic Relations

Chapter Two

QUALIFICATIONS OF DEACONS

Perfect men would be the ideal ones to elect to serve as deacons in our churches. Since perfect men are not available, there do need to be certain characteristics or qualifications for the men who are elected. No man elected to the office of deacon will possess all the Biblical qualities in perfection. However, each man elected should be a man of potential, who is yielding himself to growth in the grace and knowledge of our Lord and Savior. A saved man who has a sincere relation to the Lord and a degree of potential will grow in spiritual stature and increase his talents.

A. Essential Characteristics

There are certain essential characteristics in one chosen for a deacon. Though it is admitted that men in Acts 6 were not deacons as such, the qualifications of these men are surely characteristics which would be desired in deacons today. These are listed in verse 3: "of honest report, full of the Holy Ghost and wisdom."

1. Of honest report. These men were to have as their primary business the supervision of the financial or material matters of the church. Immediately the charitable work was placed in their hands. It was necessary that they command the complete confidence of the

people in the church and of the ones to whom they were to minister. Their good character certified by public testimony was essential to the proper accomplishment of their task. Suspicion of favoritism was already present. These men needed the complete confidence of the people.

2. Full of the Holy Ghost. All church work is spiritual. Nothing is secular in God's work. Therefore, these men needed to be full of the Holy Ghost. The term "full" is found in various passages and gives some insight into the meaning here. Jesus Himself was said to be "full of the Holy Ghost" (Luke 4:1). The Word of God is "full of grace and truth" (John 1:14). Barnabas was a man "full of the Holy Ghost and of faith" (Acts 11:24). Stephen is described as "a man full of faith and of the Holy Ghost " (Acts 6:5). According to Thayer's Greek Lexicon, the Greek word means "full, covered in every part, thoroughly permeated with, complete, lacking in nothing." To be full of the Holy Spirit means that a life is thoroughly permeated with the presence and power of the Holy Spirit. The idea speaks of complete dedication and wholehearted devotion to spiritual things.

One cannot have more or less of the Holy Spirit. Either one has the Holy Spirit or he does not have the Holy Spirit. However, the Holy Spirit can have more or less of you. The Spirit only directs that part of your life which is yielded to His control. A deacon should be yielded to the complete domination of the Spirit. Through prayer a deacon should develop such a relationship to the Holy Spirit that he knows how to perceive and follow His directions. The fullness of the Spirit in Stephen demonstrated itself in his witness (6:10) and martyrdom (7:60). The same fullness in Philip led him into extensive evangelistic work (8:5-40).

3. Full of Wisdom. The task committed to the seven required that they be competent men in administration. They needed a capability which would allow them to deal wisely in situations where human feelings had to be considered. The wisdom involved was not necessarily the wisdom of men learned through formal education. Even Paul admitted that "not many wise men after the flesh . . . are called" (1 Corinthians 1:26). Their wisdom had been born through their relationship to Christ and the indwelling of the Spirit in their lives. Men's lives are made fuller by formal learning, but there is a wisdom of a high spiritual order which is derived from a relationship to God. This wisdom is promised to all believers who desire it and ask for it (James 1:5).

4. Full of Faith. Though this characteristic is specifically ascribed only to Stephen (Acts 6:5), it is implied as an attribute of the others. Surely it is one trait that is desirable in a deacon today. The faith of Stephen was unique indeed. It appears that he had insights into the scope of the gospel which were far

beyond that of the apostles. Stephen's faith perceived how that the Lord is no respecter of persons. Peter had to learn this later (10:34), but Stephen was martyred for his faith that encompassed a gospel for all men. His faith allowed him to debate the Jews who objected to his concept of a gospel which included all men. Although that faith resulted in his life being taken, the example of that first martyr still lives. Stephen has always been an example of faith to men in difficult situations.

B. Biblical Qualifications

The specific Biblical qualifications for deacons are listed in Paul's first epistle to Timothy. Timothy was supervising the work at Ephesus. Paul was urging him to establish the leadership of the church while he was there. In this letter Paul clearly and forcefully establishes the two basic offices of the church. Only qualified men are to hold these offices. After giving the requirements for the preachers (3:1-7), Paul listed the deacons' qualifications. These are both negative and positive. Both are needed. A good leader cannot be made from all negative material. He must have some positive traits. For all of us, it is not for the actions we do not do, but for the ones which we do that we will be judged. None of these traits should be overemphasized to the exclusion of the others.

1. Grave. Gravity is a term which suggests dignity in a man. It does not refer to aloofness but to a trait in a man which makes him worthy of respect. It depicts a stately character who is serious minded about the things of God. The word was not intended to suggest a long-faced, dour man. Christians are to be a happy people. It merely means that the work of the Lord is not taken lightly. A good deacon recognizes that his work is a stewardship from God and he applies himself to it in a manner which wins respect.

2. Not Doubletongued. This is one of the negative qualities to be sought in a deacon. This word is found nowhere else in the Bible. Its plain meaning is to say one thing to one man and another thing to another person. A person who would stir discord in the church by spreading conflicting tales is not worthy to be a deacon. A deacon should be involved in visitation among members and prospects. A man who would "double-tongue" as he goes could spread havoc in a church. He cannot be trusted. He would never be adequate for the task of the deacon. Double speech with the intent to deceive is unwelcome even in worldly circles.

3. Not Given to Much Wine. Some have laughingly noted that the main distinction between the preacher and the deacon is in the fact that the preacher is "not given to wine" while the deacon is "not given to much wine." But this is a serious matter. Wine was the common beverage in that part of the world during New

Testament days. Wine is still a common drink in some nations where modern means of water purfication are not available. In such a state of affairs both preacher and deacon must be noted for their abstinence and sobriety.

This notation does not create a double standard for the minister and deacon. The whole tone of the Scriptures suggests that servants of the Lord must abstain from intoxicating drink and even the appearance of any evil connected with it. As Paul wrote the Ephesians, the believer is not to come under the influence of wine but "be filled with the Spirit" (5:18). Both the Bible and our church covenant would require that all believers abstain "from all sanction of the use and sale of intoxicating beverages." The social stigma and the terrible social evils resulting from alcoholic beverages today make it much more imperative that God's men abstain from their consumption.

4. Not Greedy of Filthy Lucre. Literally translated from the Greek, this phrase would be "not eager for base gain." Christians live in a materialistic world. Men all around them are constantly seeking for gain in any way that they can get it. The deacon generally is out in this society more than the preacher. He is to guard his testimony before others by not demonstrating an avid desire for material things. He is especially not to seek those things in a dishonorable way at the expense of others. The religious Pharisees would "devour widows'

houses" in their desire for gain (Matthew 23:14). Deacons are to be different.

5. A Strong Spiritual Life. This strong spiritual life is described by "Holding the mystery of the faith in a pure conscience" (verse 9). "Mystery" means a revealed secret. The gospel is the mystery of the faith. It is the full revelation of God through Christ Jesus. It is imperative that a disciple be a firm believer in what has been revealed in Christ. This will result in "great boldness in the faith" (verse 13). The "mystery of the faith" is referred to as "the mystery of godliness" in verse 16 and is briefly summarized there.

What a deacon believes is important because it will dictate the type of life which he lives. A firm conviction about the gospel will result in a life lived "in good conscience."

6. Proved. Novice preachers were not to be ordained (verse 6). The same holds true for deacons. The experience of this writer is that when committees are hasty in approving an untested man for either office that they are usually disappointed. Even a worthy man can sometimes be hurt by being thrust into the office before he has proved himself strong enough for the position. The concept in "proved" here is not that of a formal test or an examination. It is rather that of the testing or demonstration of one's abilities. In Galatians 6:4 Paul wrote, "Let every man prove his own work." A recent convert should never be appointed as a deacon.

The church should always be observing the men in the church. When a deacon is needed, he should be selected from among the men who have demonstrated a capability to fill the position. He does not have to be "tested." He has already proved himself to the church and they know his potential.

It is men of this type that, "being found blameless," are worthy of the office of deacon. "Blameless" does not mean perfection. Perfection is not to be found in man. The idea here is that the candidate has had no charge of wrongdoing brought against him. Observation of the man's life in the church community leaves him "unaccused" of moral evils. He can stand an impartial examination of his life.

In relation to this, another thing might be mentioned. There might be a good man in the church who was considered by most of the people to be worthy of the office but had been slandered in the community and church by vicious gossip. Although the majority of the church was persuaded of his innocence, it would not be wise to place the man in the position as long as he was not "blameless" in the eyes of all. Any man suspected of dishonesty, immorality, or any other evil would be a burden to the church and would affect its witness.

7. Good Domestic Relations. The requirements regarding home life are very similar for deacon and preacher. In relation to this, the first requirement is that

there be no record of divorce or any marital miscon-
duct. The "husband of one wife" has been interpreted
in various ways. Some have taken this to mean that the
deacon must be married. Although this is not the
meaning, the married man would generally be more
effective in his office than the unmarried man. Marriage
is the most normal state of a man, and marriage would
allow for broader relations in the church.

Others have interpreted "husband of one wife" in a
polygamous setting and interpret it to mean "the
husband of one wife at a time." Such a concept in our
modern polygamous setting would open the office to a
man of multiple divorces and this surely was not
intended by Paul.

The most natural interpretation of the phrase is
that it prohibits divorce or any other marital infidelity
in the person chosen for a deacon. Though a divorcee
may be a good man, there are complications that can
arise from his being elected to the office of deacon.
There must be nothing in a deacon's life to prohibit him
from ministering spiritually to all the people of a
community. If there is no other blame to be attached to
a divorced man, he has at least been guilty of making a
poor decision in life.

Other things are involved regarding a deacon's
home. His wife is to be qualified within the home as a
good helpmate (verse 11). Carefulness in speech,
dignity, and genuineness of faith should mark a good

deacon's wife. If her life is not in perfect balance and if
she does not abstain from hurtful things, her life will
reflect upon her husband's leadership.

The home depicts a man's real character. Paul
requires that deacons demonstrate their ability to be a
church administrator by "ruling their children and their
own houses well" (verse 12). At one time the dictatorial
nature of a father was emphasized by this clause, but it
was never intended. In a day when "obey" is taken out
of the marriage ceremony and the equality of the sexes
is stressed, the swing has been in the other direction.
But the meaning has always been the same. The rule in
the home by a good deacon will be through love and
companionship. The capacity to love and care for his
family establishes any man as the master of his home.
As he supplies their needs and leads them in spiritual
things, he establishes his rule by the help of God.

Every deacon or every man called to the office of
deacon should realize that these qualifications represent
zeal and willingness to be all that God would have him
to be. The call of a church means that the church has
faith in his potential. It does not mean that the church
believes him to be perfect. Therefore, the deacon should
pray constantly for grace from God to make him a
better leader and more fit for the office.

Chapter Three

SELECTION OF DEACONS

A. Principles Of Selection
B. Methods Of Selection
    1. The Nomination Of Deacons
    2. A Roll Of Deacons
C. Reasons For Election
D. The Deacon's Response

Chapter Three

SELECTION OF DEACONS

Preachers announce their call to the ministry, and churches give pastoral calls to those who have so set themselves forth for service. With the deacons this is not generally true. Usually the church will issue a call to a man to be a deacon, and he must then accept or refuse as he feels led by the Spirit of God. Great care needs to be taken by the church in the selection of these officials for this important office. Careful consideration should place only well-qualified men in the position. A very serious effort should be made to magnify the office through proper selection of men. It is not an honorary post to magnify a man, but a place of real service. The very name of the office implies service. A man who cannot and a man who will not serve is out of place when occupying the office. Paul said, "They that have used the office of a deacon well purchase to themselves a good degree, and great boldness in the faith which is in Christ Jesus" (1 Timothy 3:13). No honor is due the man who only bears the title.

A. Principles of Selection

The deacon is to be chosen to provide leadership for the church. His selection should be on the basis of the fact that he has already demonstrated the potential

33

for leadership. In other words, he is a "proved" man when he is elected. The deacons are to be the men in the church nearest to the needs of the people. When a man is chosen he should have already become a leader by precept and example.

Three principles especially should lead in the selection of a deacon. First, the church should engage in earnest prayer that the right man will be chosen for the office. This example of choosing leadership is exemplified in the early church. When the successor to Judas was being chosen, Luke reports that "they prayed, and said, Thou, Lord, which knowest the hearts of all men, shew whether of these two thou hast chosen" (Acts 1:24). Paul and Barnabas were sent forth as missionaries as the church at Antioch "ministered to the Lord, and fasted" (Acts 13:2). When the seven men were chosen to minister to the neglected widows, we are told that "when they had prayed, they laid their hands on them" (6:6). The deacon board, the entire church, and all individuals in the church should pray earnestly when deacons are to be chosen that God's men will be selected.

The second principle of selection is found in the Baptistic principle of congregational choice. Deacons are not to be appointed by any officer of the church nor is the final selection to be by the deacon board. This principle does not rule out the use of a committee or other means to bring names before the church. But any committee appointed should be open to consider any suggestion brought before it. Even when a committee makes its final recommendation, the floor should be open for nominations if the body so desires it. The man elected should have the unquestioned support of the church.

The third principle of selection has to do with the candidate's understanding of the responsibility which is being placed upon him. Jesus said, "No man, having put his hand to the plough, and looking back, is fit for the kingdom of God" (Luke 9:62). He also said, "For which of you, intending to build a tower, sitteth not down first, and counteth the cost, whether he have sufficient to finish it?" (Luke 14:28). Although he cannot fathom all that is involved, the pastor or one of the deacons should describe the responsibilities of the office to him.

B. Methods of Selection

Every church should have an adopted constitution and by-laws which regulates the election of all its officers. A special section should detail the manner in which deacons are elected. If a church has a method so prescribed, it will keep down many problems. When a church has no prescribed method in its constitution, the particular method of election should be decided upon in advance of the election.

1. The Nomination of Deacons. There are various methods of bringing nominees for the office before the church. One of the most common methods has been nominations from the floor. This is entirely proper in a church with the Baptistic form of government. There are definite disadvantages to this method. The main objection is found in the fact that, if a person is nominated who is not qualified, someone must rise to their feet and state an objection to the nomination. This can prove embarrassing to the nominee, his family, and the church itself. Any nominee must be considered in a frank and open manner. If this method is chosen, everyone involved must recognize that loving, but honest, discussion of the nominee and his qualifications is in order.

Nominations by the deacon board is another method used to bring nominees before the congregation. There is probably no group in the church which is more qualified to evaluate and recommend officers of the church than the board of deacons. The chief disadvantage of this method is found in fact that it makes the board of deacons a self-perpetuating body. This method might be used with no problem in most churches. However, man tends toward clannishness. The tendency for a small group perpetuating itself is to select those near to its members in various relationships. The worth of men in the total fellowship can be overlooked easily. Though the ability of deacons to choose wisely is not questioned, the wisdom of allowing them to have this authority would be questionable in most circumstances. A nominating committee representing the whole church is another way to bring nominations before the church body. Such a committee, whether elected by the congregation or appointed by the pastor, should be composed of members who will make themselves fully aware of the qualifications for a deacon. The committee should be large enough to represent the church well. It could be composed of men and women. Both the young and the old members of the church should be represented on it. The church might have a standing nominating committee. If so, this committee could be used. Its experience and knowledge of the membership would make it appropriate for this task.

Another method is the nomination of deacons by the pastor. Of course, his voice should be involved in either nominating committee or deacon board nominations. He is vitally interested in the position, because the man will be working closely with him in the leadership of the church. However, leaving the nomination of deacons up to the pastor is a big decision for the church. He does have the advantage of a knowledge of a larger number of the members of the church than any other one person. He could weigh the qualifications of all.

The chief danger in nominations by the pastor lies in the feeling that some might have that his recommendation was influenced by his personal friendship with the nominee. It also places an awesome responsibility on the pastor. If something should happen to prove his judgment wrong in the nominee, he would have to bear the stigma of a bad judgment.

One possibility is to use two steps. The pastor could make recommendation to either the deacon board or a nominating committee. After one of these groups had considered the pastor's selection, that committee in turn could make its nomination to the congregation. This would vitally associate the pastor in the selection and recommendation, yet the actual nomination to the church would be by a committee representing the body. The added step would ensure a better examination of nominees. If a nominee were rejected by the congregation, they would not be directly rejecting the pastor's nomination, but that of the committee.

Dual nominations are sometimes made by committees. This means that whoever is responsible for nominations makes two or more nominations for each position. This gives the church a definite choice. It also rules out the influence of the committee toward one man. If a committee makes a single nomination and another nomination is made from the floor, the committee nomination has a distinct advantage over the other man. But when the committee makes two nominations, neither has advantage and the majority of the church has clearly chosen the man for the office. Being nominated and not elected need not embarrass a person. He should rather count it an honor.

2. A Roll of Deacons. Some churches maintain a roll of deacons. The deacons not actively serving on the board of deacons are referred to as inactive deacons. The inactive deacons are given consideration when election of a new and active member of the board is to be selected. Election of an inactive man to the active board is generally determined by his present participation in the work and service in the church. Churches with rotating boards generally have more ordained men than are actively serving. A man is generally required to be off the active board for at least one year after each term of service. This allows a variety of men to serve the church. It also gives the church an opportunity to reject a man whose service to the church is not satisfactory. All men on the deacon roll should be honored as deacons by the church. They should be given every opportunity for service and leadership in the church, although they are not actively participating in board meetings.

C. Reasons for Election

The reasons for the nomination and election of a man should be based upon the fact that the man meets the Biblical qualifications for being a deacon. He should not be elected as a deacon just because he is a good business man. Of course, if he is a good business man and also meets all the other qualifications, this does make him highly desirable as a deacon.

Wealth is not an adequate measure of a man for the office. A man in the church who has great possessions but no spiritual qualifications should never be nominated for the position. However, a man with a lot of money should not be denied the honor of the office if he has other qualities to commend him to the office.

Men should desire the office. However, a man should never campaign for the office nor desire it inordinately. The only legitimate desire for the office is so that one may serve Christ and witness in the church. Desire for prominence in the church or the presitge of the office makes a man ineligible for the position.

No man ever deserves or merits the office because of who he is or what he has done. The committee charged with nominating men for the office should see only what potential a person has to contribute to the spiritual service of the church. Unless a man can make a spiritual contribution to leadership in the body, he has no reason for being elected as a deacon.

D. The Deacon's Response

As previously mentioned, the call of a deacon comes initially from the church. A man may have suspected that he might be called, and each man in the church should be ready to respond to the call of the church. As he considers the responsibilities of the office, each man must determine before God if He would have him serve in this capacity. The call of the church alone is not sufficient to make a man a good deacon. His own response and dedication before God will determine his effectiveness in the office.

The response of the deacon to the call of his church is a committal to service. Though the call is an honor and to an honorable position, the basic response of the man is a dedication to service in the church. The title of a deacon and the activity of the deacon as described in the New Testament always stresses his ministration to the service of the church. He should not interpret his office as one of authority but as one of servitude. His servitude is to the church and Christ. It is by self-denial and sacrifice that he will labor to see that the work of Christ is achieved through his church. Too many men elected to the office revel in the honor placed upon them and never submit themselves to the service to which they are called. A man responding to a church's call must respond with service.

The response of a man to the call of the church must be to another heavy responsibility. That is the burden of being an example to others. Just as with the pastor, so much more is expected of the deacon than of the ordinary member. He is watched by all. His attendance is noted. His devotion and loyalty to the programs of the church are carefully noted. His stewardship of time, money, and talents is an example to every other member. Even his attitudes are weighed carefully in every situation. Thus, a man responding to the call of the church must accept the pressure of being watched by others. He must be willing to walk and talk an example for others.

Chapter Four

THE SERVICE OF ORDINATION

A. The Meaning Of Ordination
   1. The Recognition Of Fitness
   2. The Dignity Of The Office
   3. An Expression Of Benediction
B. The Service Itself
   1. A Charge To The Church
   2. The Charge To The Deacon
   3. Response By The Deacon
   4. The Prayer Of Consecration
   5. The Laying On Of Hands
C. Procedures
D. Suggested Service Of Ordination

Chapter Four

THE SERVICE OF ORDINATION

Men called to the office of deacon are generally "ordained" for that office. The ordination for the service in some areas is carried out by the quarterly meeting or district association. In some areas the church itself plans and directs the service completely independent of these bodies. In yet other areas the quarterly meeting or district association questions and approves the candidates and the ordination service is left to the local church. In a congregational type government it is best for the local church to exercise the greatest liberty in the selection and ordination of its leaders.

A. The Meaning of Ordination

The service of ordination which usually climaxes with the laying on of the hands of the other ordained minsters and deacons is purely a symbolic service. Free Will Baptists do not believe that the laying on of hands confers any special power upon the deacon. The laying on of hands might be compared to baptism. Baptism confers no power and makes no change in the individual. Submission to baptism by a person is to give to the world an outward sign of the inward change which has been experienced by the believer. The ordination of a deacon confers no inward power but is a token of the setting apart of the candidate by the church for service.

By the laying on of hands three things are expressed:

1. The Recognition of Fitness. The ordination ceremony speaks to those present and tells them that the church recognizes the fitness of the candidate for this office. It is the formal recognition of qualities in the person to perform the duties of this office.

2. The Dignity of the Office. The ordination service dignifies the office. The election of a deacon is more than just the election of any officer. It is one of the two divinely appointed offices of the New Testament and deserves a recognition above other offices. The man involved is giving up many privileges to dedicate himself to service. He is setting himself up as an example in the church. The church is recognizing his fitness for service. It is only appropriate that such a dedication be dignified by a special service.

3. An Expression of Benediction. The service is an invocation of a blessing from God upon the new officer. The church in this symbolic service is asking God to bless the deacon in the ministry which he is now assuming. The deacon has committed his life to service to God and his church. As he enters this new relationship, it is imperative that he do so with the blessing of God upon his ministry. Such a spiritual ministry as he now assumes can only be performed by the grace and help of God.

B. The Service Itself

The call of the deacon comes from the local church. His selection was by the people of the church where he sustains his membership. It is in this local church that his service of ordination should be held. Since the ordination dignifies the office and places him before the people in order to emphasize his responsibilities, the service should be well planned to give both recognition and instruction. The people should be impressed with the office and its responsibilities.

The example for ordination comes from the New Testament. The laying on of hands is exemplified in the choosing and setting apart of the seven men for service in Acts 6:1-8. The service is described briefly in these words: "When they had prayed, they laid their hands on them" (verse 6). A similar service was held for the first missionaries sent out by the church. The report from the service at the church in Antioch reads, "And when they had fasted and prayed, and laid their hands on them, they sent them away" (Acts 13:3). Again let it be emphasized that no special power was imparted by the laying on of hands. It is a symbol of the setting apart for a special ministry. Deacons and ministers alike have been dedicated to their service by this symbolic action.

The service of ordination should be held in conjunction with one of the main services of the church. This will ensure that a representative group of the

members will be present. Since the service will be both
instructional and inspirational, the church membership
should be involved. The whole service should be
conducted in a lively, spiritual atmosphere to dignify
and magnify the office. Both dignity and sincerity
should be felt since this is a sacred moment to the
deacon and should be to the whole church as well.

The message in the service may or may not be
related to the ordination service. If the total service is
given over to the ordination, it would give the pastor or
a visiting speaker a good opportunity to preach a
challenging message to all the deacons present. However,
the ordination may be held before or after the regular
service of the church.

Several elements that should be in the ordination
service itself are as follows:

1. A Charge to the Church. This is a sacred
moment to the church. It too has responsibilities to the
man who is being set aside for a ministry. The church
needs to be charged anew concerning the relations
which exist between the deacon and the church. If this
man is committing himself to a sacrificial ministry in the
church, surely the church must commit itself to support
him in prayer and response to his leadership and
example.

2. The Charge to the Deacon. The charge to the
deacon is one of the key elements in the service. This is
a good time for the one giving the charge to make a clear

statement of the duties of the office. The deacon himself should already have been made aware of those duties. But an explanation of those duties before the church will be instructive to the members and make them aware of the responsibilities of the office.

3. Response by the Deacon. Though it is not necessary, a moment of response and testimony by the deacon could be allowed. A moment for a word of acceptance of the responsibility of the office would give him opportunity to solicit the support of the church as he performed his duties.

4. The Prayer of Consecration. The prayer of consecration should be specifically directed to the purpose of the service. The one praying should lead the church in its dedication to the support of the new deacon. The new deacon should be presented to God for His care and guidance in the performance of his work. Of course, the candidate himself would silently be dedicating himself to the office and the service it demands.

5. The Laying on of Hands. The most directly scriptural part of the service is the prayer and the laying on of hands. This laying on of hands is done by the ordained ministers and deacons who are present. No spiritual power is bestowed. Let this be remembered. It symbolizes the church's recognition of abilities in this man to perform the office. It pledges their support and encouragement in his duties. The laying on of hands

should be followed by a hand of fellowship given by the members of the church and also by all Christians who are present. The whole body expresses their support to the man in his new service.

C. Procedures.

The pastor of the church should be in charge of the service and plan the service. If he so desires, he may plan the service with the board of deacons and the man or men to be ordained. If the message is to be related to the service, the pastor can bring the message. For added emphasis, an outside speaker could be invited for the occasion.

Usually a variety of persons is used for the different parts of the service. Other members of the deacon board can be used for the prayer, the charge, and so on. A pastor might prefer to let the candidate choose a former pastor or some deacon or preacher close to him to be involved in some phase of the service. This is not necessary, and often the service is held as a purely local church function with no advertisement to other churches. Usually, however, the candidate will desire to have relatives and friends present for this special moment in his life.

The laying on of hands may be carried out in a variety of ways. Where a council from an association is in charge of the service, the members of the council often will kneel with the candidate and lay their hands on him during the prayer. At the close of the prayer, they rise and lay their hands gently on his head one by one as he remains kneeling. If other ordained men have been kneeling in the altar, they are often invited to rise and follow this procedure.

If the service is held in the local church under the direction of the pastor (and this is to be preferred), he and the other deacons in the church should kneel near the candidate. If they desire, they may place their hands upon the candidate during the prayer. Other ordained men could be invited to kneel around them. After the prayer the pastor should rise and lay his hands gently upon the man's head. The deacons of that local church should follow the pastor's example. Then the visiting ordained men could follow them.

D. Suggested Service of Ordination

1. Charge to the Church
2. Charge to the Deacon
3. Response of the Deacon
4. Prayer of Dedication
5. Laying on of Hands
6. The Hand of Fellowship
7. Concluding Prayer

Chapter Five

A DEACON'S RELATIONSHIPS

A. To The Pastor
B. To Other Officials
C. To The Membership
D. To The World

Chapter Five

A DEACON'S RELATIONSHIPS

The board of deacons will be related to the total work of the church. Either by example or direct association, they will affect every phase of the work. Only the most vital areas of contact can be outlined in this chapter.

A. To the Pastor

The relation of deacons to the pastor will necessarily be a close one. These are the two divinely appointed offices in the New Testament church and were set up for the watch-care of the membership. The church will only progress in the work of the Lord as these two offices harmonize their efforts. The board of deacons was never intended to lord it over the pastor. Neither is the pastor a dictator over the board of deacons. The pastor is the elected leader of the church. The office of deacon has been created to give assistance to the pastor. There is an interrelation between the two offices. The pastor does not order the deacons. The pastor accepts them as co-workers in the area of pastoral leadership. As he confides in the deacons and relies upon them for service, they recognize his leadership and follow his counsel in the work of the church.

The pastor's thought, time, and energies are devoted to the chief areas of service and leadership. The deacons are to assume the execution of the details of the work. The pastor cannot be a one-man army. He needs the deacons to follow his leadership in the accomplishment of the service of the church.

Free Will Baptists have had a real problem in the area of pastor-deacon relationships because of the nature of our churches. The churches have been chiefly rural in most states and have been served by pastors who most often did not reside in the church community. As a result of this, a deacon has become *the* leader in the church. Through the years his leadership has become established because of his service in the church. The pastor, coming into the community once or twice a week, performs the necessary tasks of the preacher but generally has not assumed leadership of the church in its business affairs. When a church with such a situation calls a resident or full-time pastor, it is not easy for the deacon to relinquish his role as leader. Oftentimes friction in leadership roles results and the pastor is the loser.

Since Free Will Baptist churches are still in transition to full-time pastorates across the land, strong deacons need to be aware of the impact of their leadership. When a pastor is elected as the leader in the church, deacons need to recognize the leadership of the pastor and follow him. In many of our churches across the land, strong deacon leadership has continued after churches have called full-time pastors. Deacons in these churches continue to dominate the church regardless of who is called as pastor. Such churches become known for the rapid turnover in its pastors. Usually a pastor can serve only until his policies come in conflict with the dominant deacon. Then he has to move. In defense of deacons, let it be remembered that their actions are generally sincere and without rancor. Pastors often precipitate a crisis by not being patient and serving until their influence becomes strong enough to lead the church membership. Division often grows out of a pastor's jealousy of a good deacon's influence. However, deacons need to be careful and respect the pastor's leadership.

As long as a preacher is the pastor of a church, deacons have no right to undermine his work. Unless the pastor is guilty of some immoral act or unchristian conduct, the pastor is due the support of the deacons in the church. When dissatisfaction with some action of the pastor arises, deacons should never perpetuate a division in the church because of it. Rather they should be adult and mature enough to go to the pastor and discuss the matter openly.

There should be a perfect confidence existing between pastor and deacons in the church. A pastor becomes many ministers as he works through his deacons. They are his means of executing and enlarging his ministry. A fruitful church is not one with a pastor who labors unceasingly, but a church in which pastor and deacons serve as a team.

B. To Other Officials

The relation of the deacons to other officials in the church will depend upon the constitution and by-laws of the local church. In some churches the constitution of the church has established an official board which is composed of other leaders along with the deacons. In such instance the administrative work of the church is left to this official board. Unless this is otherwise spelled out, however, the board of deacons with the pastor makes up the official administrative board of the church.

Although the Scriptures assign no particular services to the deacons, the business of the church has generally fallen into their hands. It is an area of church work where they can render an effective service.

The trustees will supervise the work which is accorded them by the constitution and by-laws of the church. Usually they are merely the legal channel through which the church holds title to property. Some churches entrust to them the care and maintenance of the church property. This needs to be clearly spelled out so there will be no conflict with the board of deacons. Usually expansion, improvements, or new property fall under the duties of the deacons where they are the official board of the church.

If the board of deacons serves as the budget committee of the church, they should consult with and work very closely with the treasurer of the church. To relieve the pastor of such a responsibility, the deacons could supervise the work of the ushers. A music committee from the board of deacons could serve well in supervising the music program of the church. Whenever the church has a board of Christian education, the deacons could act with them to get every member involved in some task in the church. Every member should be considered as available manpower and his talent should be utilized by the church.

The teaching and training ministries of the church should get the attention of the board of deacons. Consultations with the Sunday school superintendent and the Church Training Service director would encourage them and coordinate their work with the total ministry of the church. These two leaders should present to the board of deacons the business they have to bring before the church.

The seven men appointed in Acts 6 were to serve tables of benevolence. The office of deacon was established for a much broader service than this. Though these men should be men of sharp business and financial judgment, they should remember that their chief function is in the area of spiritual matters. Promoting the general harmony of the church should be the chief desire of each deacon.

C. To the Membership

The deacon is to remember that he is always a church member among church members. His ordination gave him no special right of access to God or no peculiar power above others. He is distinguished from other members only in the sense that his leadership has been specially acknowledged by the group.

The deacon should be a member of each organization in the church which is designed for him. His example in being a member of the Sunday school, the CTS, and the Master's Men is the least that he can do. He should be present when these meet and support their work. His absence, unless he is unable to attend, is a vote against this phase of church work. By participating in each auxiliary, he is brought into close contact with the individual members of the church.

The promotion of fellowship in the church is a privilege of deacons. The early church was a fellowship more than an organization. It should still be so. People who are saved should enter a fellowship of believers. The deacons can be a key to the promotion of this fellowship. It needs to be an open fellowship that leaves no believer on the outside. When cliques form or a church becomes clannish, it begins to die. It is good to be close to a group in the church. But when a group becomes so close in its fellowship that all are not welcome in it, the true spirit of Christian fellowship has been lost. Deacons should labor to keep the fellowship of the church open to all. More will be discussed about the deacon's relationship to church members in the chapter on the spiritual welfare of members.

D. To the World

One of the qualifications for a bishop given by Paul was that "he must have a good report of them which are without" (1 Timothy 3:7). Although this is not specifically stated to be a requirement for a deacon, it is implied. The seven men in Acts 6 were to be "men of honest report." The deacons will be the church contact with men in the business and financial world. It is imperative that they observe the highest Christian principles in dealing with men outside the church. The ethics of Jesus should be applied in every transaction of the church. The testimony of the church is at stake.

The deacon is a layman and as such will be working and living each day in the environment of the world. Since he is a marked man as an officer in the church, he must guard his reputation carefully. The average layman might live in sin without any great reflection on the church. But when a deacon hurts his testimony by any ungodly action, the image of the church suffers greatly in the community.

The influence of the deacon should be a positive Christian one before the world. By a good Christian testimony he should witness to the world for Christ and seek to win men to Him. If he gives no positive witness, he will have no influence as a Christian leader. Through a positive witness men will come to respect him, his Savior, and the church.

Chapter Six

ORGANIZATION OF THE BOARD

A. Structure Of The Board
B. Meetings Of The Board
C. The Training Of Deacons

Chapter Six

ORGANIZATION OF THE BOARD

The deacon belongs to an unusual group of men. These are men who have been recognized by their church and set apart for specific leadership. Acceptance of the call of the church has placed them in the group. The individual deacon should recognize that he is not an individual who acts alone but a part of a group that must act together in its official duties.

A. Structure of the Board

The number of men on the board of deacons should not be governed by the number of men selected in Acts 6. There seven men were needed to fill a need so seven were selected. Each church needs to determine the number of men needed as deacons and select that number. Each church should determine the ratio of deacons to membership that it should have and follow that ratio. There definitely should not be as many deacons in a church of one hundred members as there is in a church with one thousand members.

The office of the deacon is a service office and not an honor office. The demands of that service should control the number of deacons elected. If a deacon has specific oversight of a group of members, one deacon to every twenty-five families would be a big task. The number of resident church families should be the determining factor in the number selected.

Another factor in determining the number of deacons will be the number of qualified men who are available. A church should never elect men just to have a certain number on the board. If qualified and capable men are not immediately available, the church should wait until they are qualified and willing to serve.

Each church should structure its board so that the men rotate in the office. Nothing is more stifling to the work of the church than "lifetime" deacons. A church would not think of electing a perpetual pastor. It is very difficult to remove a deacon for any reason in a church where deacons are elected to the board until they die. A church should so constitute its deacon board so that each man comes up for re-election after a term of years. This gives the church an opportunity to judge a man's work and weigh his continued usefulness to the church. It also opens the way for better qualified and more capable men to be elected to the board.

Various systems of rotation can be used. A church with seven deacons (or a multiple of seven) could have seven year terms. One man would be up for election each year. If a three year term were desired by the church, any multiple of three could be elected each year and a board of any size based on a multiple of three could be constituted.

Some churches require a deacon to be off the

board for at least one year after his term of service before he is eligible for re-election. A true rotation plan will require this if the church expects to benefit from this plan. No man should automatically return to the board. It should be understood that the way is always open for selection of new men to the board. The year off will give the deacon an opportunity to fill positions that he might not be able to fill due to his work as a deacon. No man should serve longer than seven years at one time. Three or five year terms are preferable.

Deacons who move their membership from one church to another do not automatically become a member of the board at the new church to which they move their membership. The fact of their ordination should be noted on their church letter. Their recognition as a deacon should be granted in the new church. However, their selection as an active deacon on the board must await election to the office by the church. In the case of churches that do not have a rotating system, a deacon from another church does not automatically become an active deacon by merely joining the church. His ordination should be recognized, but his participation on the board will only come when the church sees fit to elect him to the board. As a way of illustration, sometimes several preachers belong to a church. However, only one is recognized as the pastor. On church letters the others would be listed as ordained ministers belonging to the church, but they would never be listed as pastor until elected by the church.

The board of deacons should be organized with at least three officers: chairman, vice-chairman, and secretary. The chairman should preside at all meetings of the board, or the vice-chairman in his absence. The secretary of the board should keep good records of the meetings.

Any member of the board should be fit to serve as chairman. In some boards the person who will be going off the board that year is designated as chairman. In other boards he is elected by the board. In all cases the chairman is assuming a great reponsibility. Because of the great responsibility, the position should not stay on one man's shoulders for any great length of time.

The chairman of the board will be working closely with the pastor and will be sensing the needs in the church program in a special way. He should feel a special concern for the attendance of the other deacons at the meeting. He should keep aware of the attendance record of the other deacons at worship and auxiliary services. If negligence becomes apparent in the life of another deacon, he should be the first to sit down and counsel with him and to advise him of his responsibilities. The chairman is the right hand man of the pastor and his source of encouragement.

When a deacon board in a church becomes large enough, committees should be set up to give attention to various aspects of the work. Temporary committees ought to be appointed to meet particular needs.

Committees can be used to save time on vital matters as they look into details and report back to the board.

B. Meetings of the Board

The meetings of the board of deacons should be planned carefully and set at a regular time. At least once a month meetings of the board should be held even if the meeting is only for fellowship. The meetings should be planned so that each deacon can attend.

The convenient time of meeting will not be the same in all churches. A Monday evening is good in some churches. However, when some of the deacons of a church work outside the community during the week, a weekend meeting is necessary. A Saturday night meeting is required when some deacons work at night during the week. The important thing is to set the time for the convenience of the deacons. A man who cannot arrange his plans to attend the meetings should not be elected to the active board. Once a time of meeting is set, it should not be altered except upon special occasions. If the meeting time is constantly changed, respect for its importance will be lost. The church should be aware of the meeting time and other activities requiring the presence of the deacons should not be planned to conflict with their meetings.

Each deacon has the responsibility to be present at

every meeting unless providentially hindered. A deacon who regularly absents himself from the meetings of the board shows that he considers other things more important than his calling to this office.

The chairman of the deacon board should work out a program or agenda for every meeting of the board. He should see that the meeting begins on time and that the agenda is carefully followed. A time should be planned for reports on the various aspects of the church work and also planning for the future. A well-planned program will make the other deacons aware of a need to meet. Generally speaking, about one hour will suffice for time in a well-coordinated meeting. Longer meetings will be necessary when certain matters such as expansion programs are being considered. The meeting should be concise and business like. When the business is concluded, the meeting should be adjourned for fellowship.

The business of the church should be handled in the regular deacons' meeting. If a matter arises demanding the attention of the deacons, the board should be convened for a meeting. Handling church business over the telephone or mouth-to-mouth by a partial board can lead to ill results. Misunderstandings arise. It is a dangerous custom for a partial board to handle matters also.

C. The Training of Deacons

Ministers receive training. Sunday school teachers are trained. Why should deacons not also be trained? Someone described the average church as "a mob with a pastor trying to bring order and discipline into the midst of undisciplined people." This is somewhat extreme, but does typify some local situations. The deacons of the church need to be aware of their duties and how to perform them. There is no better way to train them than to set up a training course for deacons. A deacon should be willing to spend some time in learning these duties and how to perform them. Even though they have held the office for years with no training, deacons should not resent a pastor who desires to better equip them for their position.

Small churches which have only a few deacons could cooperate in an associational training class for deacons. One pastor could teach the whole course, or each pastor in the area could talk on selected areas of the deacon's work.

The ideal situation would be for the individual pastor to hold a training course in his church each year for the deacons in the church. These could be held separately or in conjunction with other officer training courses (such as ushers, teachers, and so forth). Four or five sessions of an hour each should be sufficient for this instruction. These could precede or follow one of the regularly scheduled services such as evening worship or the midweek prayer service. Qualifications, duties, and responsibilities should be stressed in these sessions.

Probably the lack of understanding of their duties has hindered deacons more than anything else in their work. Deacons are generally sincere and honest men who desire to serve. Most churches have no outlined duties or responsibilities for their boards of deacons. The church and pastor owe it to the deacons to clarify what is expected of them. When this is done, it becomes the obligation of the individual deacon to serve as the church has directed.

Chapter Seven

RESPONSIBILITIES AND DUTIES

A. A Spiritual Service
B. Church Administration
C. Worship Services

RESPONSIBILITIES AND DUTIES

Custom and tradition in various areas have laid an assortment of duties upon deacons. Many duties have been assumed by deacons because the church has not been specific in its assignment of responsibilities to them. Anyone who takes a job or position always wants to know what is expected of him. So each church needs to be clear and specific in what it expects from its deacons. In reality the Scriptures describe no particular duties to the deacon which are exclusively his. The Scriptures do give intimations as to what his duties are.

A. A Spiritual Service

The Free Will Baptist *Treatise* gives only a general description of the duties of deacons (page 50). It says, "Deacons, who are ordained—usually by the local church—[are] to minister to the congregation and exercise general spiritual leadership. They assist the pastor in administering the ordinances, and may have to conduct worship services in the pastor's absence." There are two general duties assigned here: (1) to minister to the congregation; and (2) to exercise general spiritual leadership.

These two general duties are comparable to the duties assigned the "seven" in Acts 6. Those men were

to minister specifically to one segment of the church—
the neglected widows. However, they were also to give
spiritual leadership in another area. There was a rift in
the ranks of the church fellowship. Gentile converts and
Hebrew Christians were at odds with each other. These
men were to solve the problem which threatened the
unity of the body. Thus the task of the deacons
transcended the immediate responsibility of serving
tables.

The work of the deacon should never be thought
of as being over the "secular" matters of the church
while the pastor is over the "spiritual." To the believer
nothing is "secular" in his work for Christ. If the
deacons were assigned only duties in regard to the
finance of the church, it should be remembered that
finances come within the area of stewardship. No phase
of Christian activity is more spiritual than the act of
giving one's tithes and offerings to the Lord in worship.
The responsibility of spending that money is also a
spiritual service.

The duties, therefore, of the deacons merge with
those of the pastor. The deacons are to serve as the right
hand men of the pastor. They should be a constant
source of encouragement and strength to him. Deacons
are the staff or assistants of the pastor to minister in
whatever capacities their talents or the opportunities
make possible. Both pastor and deacon are ministering
servants in the church. The two offices constitute the

"ministering" group in the church.

There is no conflict when we say that these two offices "serve" and "lead" the church. Did not our Lord say, "Whosoever of you will be the chiefest, shall be servant of all" (Mark 10:44)? The pastor was never intended to be the "boss" of the deacon board and church. He is elected to be the leader and chief minister of the church. The deacon board was never intended to be the "boss" of the pastor and church. They are selected to serve under the pastor as co-leaders and fellow ministers. For this reason deacons have an important responsibility in the spiritual leadership of the congregation.

The duties of pastor and deacon will often overlap. This makes it important for each deacon to study and practice the fine art of cooperation with the pastor and other deacons. Lest they mar their spiritual influence, deacons must manifest Christian courtesy, wisdom, and tact in all their activities.

Recognizing the leadership of the pastor and following his counsel, the deacons perform the duties placed upon them in the highest possible spiritual manner. By executing the details of the service which would absorb the pastor's thought and time, they relieve the pastor for more pressing requirements in his office. By being spiritual leaders among the members and by ministering to the needs of the church membership, deacons become a cohesive force in the church which binds it together for its total ministry. It is in this general spiritual ministry that deacons perform their greatest service.

B. Church Administration

In actual church administration deacons also assist the pastor in the ministry of the church. Deacons are usually among the most able men in financial and business judgment. As owners of property and as actual participants in the business world, these men are especially equipped to guide the business matters of the church. Many pastors, who generally are not experienced in these matters, have been saved from serious mistakes through the advice and good judgment on the part of their deacons.

Although no man is qualified as a deacon simply because of his possession of wealth or business ability, these qualities are assets in the lives of men called to be deacons. If a man has the spiritual qualifications, it is good when he has the added talents of administrative and financial abilities.

In the administration of a church the deacon board should be involved in the overall planning of the church program. Every other facet of the work should be carried out under the supervision of the pastor and deacons. The planning of the total work and the supervision should be centered in these officers.

Long range programs such as building and expansion especially should be the particular work of the board of deacons. Any recommendations to the church should come from them for adding to or enlarging the church plant. Any improvements in the property should be brought before the church by the board of deacons.

The basic program of the church as it is related to the organized activities of the church to accomplish its basic purpose is also the domain of the board of deacons. This purpose is the accomplishment of the Great Commission (Matthew 28:18-20). The deacon board, again under the leadership of the pastor, should plan the program of the church so that its energies are used to accomplish this commission. Further treatment of the main aspects of this program will be discussed in the next chapter.

In regard to church property more and more churches are recognizing the deacons as trustees of the church. Trustees generally are the legal channels through which the church holds title or transfers property. If a church takes this step in designating the deacons as trustees, it probably would also entrust to them the care and maintenance of the property as well. Some churches which have a separate board of trustees designate them merely as legal channels for holding title to the property and leave the care and maintenance of the property in the hands of the deacon board. This needs to be clearly spelled out by the individual church in its constitution and by-laws. Many problems have arisen in churches because of a lack of clarification in these duties.

The deacon, like the pastor, should have an intense concern for all that is going on in the church. He should make it his business to know what is going on. This will allow him in the meetings of the deacons and pastor to make wise decisions with the other leaders as they plan the overall program of the church and administer it. Deacons are the men who should have the vision of God in expansion of the total church program: Without a vision, the people perish.

C. Worship Services

The deacons have an important part to play in making the services of worship have meaning to all the other members. The physical surroundings, assisting the pastor in the arrangements for the service, seeing that the ushering is carried out properly, and soliciting the attendance of the members are all a part of the duties of deacons.

The preparation of the sanctuary for the service is a duty of the deacons. Although the church may have an attendant, the arrangement of chairs or any change for a particular service should be cared for by the deacons.

The comfort of the worshipers is necessary if the participants are to get the most out of the service. The deacons should see to it that the temperature is properly controlled. Deacons should see to it that visiting mothers with babies know where the nursery facilities are located.

There should be very little movement in the sanctuary during a worship service. Seeing to it beforehand that the speakers are turned on, that the lights are properly adjusted, and that the hymnbooks are within the reach of everyone can eliminate distracting movements after the service begins.

Individual pastors will work with their deacons in different ways. Some pastors like to have prayer with the deacon board. Others have prayer with the choir since deacons are often in the choir. A very impressive thing is for the deacons to come into the service after prayer and all sit on the front pew of the church. This gives the pastor the confidence of their united support during the service. It also makes them readily available for altar work. There is the added advantage of improving their attendance at the service since an absence would be conspicuous. Another feature is the recognition that it gives to the office of deacon.

The act of making people welcome at the service is not one for the pastor alone. The deacons should circulate among the people and exert some effort in welcoming members and visitors alike. The kind of experience people have in their reception at a church determines whether they return or not. Just to introduce oneself to visitors can serve to make them feel welcome. Greeting all that they can enables the deacons to build the atmosphere of a friendly church. Friendliness and a happy fellowship can be nurtured by an active board of deacons. Greeting of visitors left to an unorganized method usually means that it will not be done.

The pastor directs the service and fills the pulpit when present. The conduct of the service is the priority of the pastor. The subject matter of the sermons is between him and the Lord. When the pastor is absent, the deacons are usually given the ministration of the service. If the pastor has a planned absence, he will generally secure a speaker and appoint one of the deacons to conduct or lead the service. Should the pastor have to miss the service unexpectedly due to illness or accident, the deacons should assume the responsibility for filling the pulpit in his absence. In some instances the deacons themselves could fill the pulpit and speak.

A great responsibility falls upon the board of deacons when a pastor resigns or the church is otherwise without the services of a pastor. Unless the church elects a pulpit committee especially for the task, it is the responsibility of the deacons to see that the pulpit is filled temporarily and to work toward securing a new pastor.

The pastor of a church generally administers the ordinances of the church. The deacons should see to it that the pastor has every assistance to make the ordinances meaningful. At each baptismal service, the deacons should see to it that the baptistry is filled, if the church has one. Some churches still use streams of water or lakes. If so, the deacons should see that the site of the service is in order. At least one deacon should accompany the pastor to the edge of the baptistry to offer any assistance possible such as holding towels or otherwise assisting the candidates.

At the Lord's Supper the deacons will serve with the pastor as the pastor directs in serving the elements of the Supper. The deacons should see that the elements are prepared and the table ready before the service begins. The deacons should have rooms prepared for the feet washing service and have a good supply of water, pans, and towels for men and women. The care of the towels and pans should be supervised by the deacons.

The first essential of every worship service is to have the deacons in attendance. By being present, they can serve various functions. Their attendance then permits them to urge others to attend. The securing of a house full of worshipers is one of the chief responsibilities of the deacons. This task is often assumed by the pastor because the deacons neglect it. But he is to fill the pulpit; the deacons, the pews. The deacons should work constantly to build attendance at worship by bringing in the people.

Chapter Eight

THE SPIRITUAL WELFARE OF MEMBERS

A. Nurture And Culture
B. Benevolent Work
C. A Unit System Of Watchcare

Chapter Eight

THE SPIRITUAL WELFARE OF MEMBERS

As previously mentioned, the work of the deacon is chiefly a spiritual ministry. That ministry should affect the whole church as the deacon ministers to the spiritual needs of all the church community. Not only should the pastor be looked to in the community as a counselor and spiritual guide, but each deacon should be so respected as well.

A. Nurture and Culture

A deacon is not full-time in the sense that the pastor is, but each deacon should give a steward's portion of his time to the nurture and culture of the members. If a man meets the qualifications of being a deacon, he has the talents, abilities, and spiritual power to be a blessing in the church body. As these lay leaders contribute a share of their best effort to serving the spiritual needs of the church, the rank and file members will be brought to much greater productivity as Christians.

The deacons should call upon the sick. This is an essential and helpful part of their work. These calls can be very brief. The callers should go with a cheerful spirit, have a brief prayer, and leave behind a spirit of love and good-will. This ministry of the deacons could be extended to non-members as well as members. This will build up the work of the Lord outside the church. The deacon can give the names of the more necessary calls to the pastor for his visits.

Deacons should be looked to for help by the troubled in the community. Just as the pastor comes to be called upon for help in difficult times, so the deacons should develop a reputation as a means of assistance in troubled periods of life. Just as the aides of Moses brought their most pressing problems to Moses, so deacons should take those problems they cannot solve to the pastor.

New members are glad to have a visit from the pastor, but a visit from one of the deacons gives contact with the lay members of the church. Visitors to the church may expect a call from the pastor; but when a deacon shows his interest, it more than doubly demonstrates the interest of the church in people.

It is vitally important for deacons to recognize their spiritual ministry in regard to the nurture and culture of members. It is easy for deacons to assume the responsibility of church business. Their leadership here often overshadows their greater calling to serve the spiritual needs of the church. But in the church where the deacons assume this greater role, the whole church profits from their spiritual labors. Their interest in straggling members, their care for the neglected, their concern for the fallen boy or girl, and their witness to the lost are elements that develop a great church. It is true that these are pastoral concerns. But the pastor can do only so much. Unless his ministry is multiplied by the spiritual ministry of the deacons, the membership will not grow in spiritual stature as it should. The lack of growth in membership, the faltering loyalty to a church, and the disinterest of our youth can all be traced to a lack of dedicated service on the part of the total leadership of the church. A great pastor cannot bear the total load of the feeding of the flock. The board of deacons should be his strength and help in the culture of the members. The deacons have an opportunity for a vast investment of time and effort in their tasks. It is a sacrificial job. But the rewards are great and wonderful experiences can result (1 Timothy 3:13).

B. Benevolent Work

The church has always been a center of concern for the physical needs of man. It was to care for the needs of poor widows that the seven were appointed in Acts 6. Even before this the church had pooled its resources to face critical times (Acts 2:44, 45; 4:34, 35). Many references are made elsewhere in the Scriptures to sharing with the needy (1 John 3:17; Matthew 19:21; 25:35-45). Paul made caring for the poor saints in Jerusalem one of his specific ministries (1 Corinthians

16:1-3; 2 Corinthians 9:1-15; Romans 15:25; Acts 11:29, 30).

In our United States the care of the poor has been assumed by various charitable organizations, welfare agencies, and the government. It should be remembered that Christianity has led the way in this, and that these agencies exist because of Christian concern and influence.

Assistance on a broad scale by denominational and interdenominational groups continues today. Although local churches do not generally carry on active benevolent programs, they should continue to be sensitive to needs of people within the fellowship of the church. The church does not have the staff nor means to minister to transients, nor to determine their needs. However, the church does have many opportunities to share the needs of members and people of the immediate community.

The deacons should be the church leaders in benevolent work in the local church. The church should provide some funds for this area of need. This type of work must be handled with great care and efficiency. The church or the board of deacons should determine the basis upon which assistance will be given, the amount in each case, and for how long the assistance will continue. Whether the assistance will be confined to members or extended to other Christians and even non-Christians needs to be a set policy. A good rule to follow would be to keep the assitance confidential. This will solve many problems.

The rule for Christians is given by Paul in Galatians 6:5: "For every man shall bear his own burden." Each man is to provide for his own needs. However, without contradicting this, Paul in that same chapter had written the command, "Bear ye one another's burdens, and so fulfil the law of Christ" (verse 2). The "burdens" here are the overloads and emergencies of life. It is the aiding of men facing the overburden with which the deacons are to be concerned. When extra heavy needs fall upon a family, they suffer in many ways. The spiritual life is often threatened by physical and financial needs. Thus when the deacons minister to such needs, the spiritual needs should also be a matter of great concern. Any benevolent work done should be in the name of Christ and the church. It should be done in a way to reflect the fact that God through His servants is filling the needs of the ones involved. No individual should reap praise from church benevolent work.

C. A Unit System of Watchcare

The nurture and culture of members and their spiritual needs will not be cared for if no system is developed through which responsibility is given to specific individuals. Most Free Will Baptist churches have been small and the total watchcare of the membership has been given to the pastor. This may be one of the reasons for our lack of growth in many areas. Churches should give consideration to some type of systematic watchcare utilizing the deacons to see that the needs of the whole membership of the church are met. Worldwide and local tensions are constantly bringing more stresses into the lives of families and individuals. The church needs to be organized to watch over and give guidance to every person falling within the scope of its labor and ministry.

It would be good for our churches to adopt group plans by which deacons are given a definite assignment to minister to the needs of a certain number of members each year. These could be assigned by age groups, mutual interests, or location in an area. Assignment by families would probably be the most logical way. They could be assigned by random or the pastor could attempt to decide assignments by which deacon he felt could best meet the needs of a family. These assignments should be changed annually to allow deacons to be acquainted with a larger number of the members.

In such a system the deacon is made responsible to visit regularly each family under his watchcare. He would observe their attendance at the services of the church and be aware of any continued absences on their part. By having a definite plan of visitation, it would ensure contact of every family with the church on a regular basis. If it did nothing more than nurture fellowship, it would be worth the effort. But by feeling responsible for certain families, the deacons would keep aware of any spiritual needs in the families of the church. This system will in time develop a reliance by the people on the deacons for spiritual help.

Other benefits can accrue from this program. Through his visitation the deacon will come to learn a lot about the members under his watchcare. Often he will discover hidden talents that can be utilized in the church. Choir members, teachers, and other leaders can be discovered by acquaintance with members.

As soon as a new member is received, he should be placed on the list of one of the deacons. The deacon himself or someone whom he assigns should give special care to orientate the new member into the church work. It should be stressed to the new member that joining the church is just the initial step to service. The example and influence of the deacon can lead the new member into active participation in every phase of the church program. New members are looking for fellowship. This contact and follow-up by the deacon could provide this need.

The program of membership assignment would ensure that the sick and aged would be visited on a regular basis. Deacons could visit shut-ins on a regular basis. This would mean that Christian fellowship would be guaranteed to these. Bible reading, prayer, and good cheer need to be supplied to all confined members. The temporarily ill or shut-in could be served in the same way.

Every visit by a deacon should give evidence of a purpose. To dispense information on the aims, opportunities, or services of the church is always a good reason for a visit. To announce some special promotion is another. But the needs and growth of each member should always be uppermost in the minds of the visiting deacons.

Chapter Nine

MISSIONS AND EVANGELISM

A. A Deacon's Personal Witness
B. The Visitation Program
C. The Missions Program

Chapter Nine

MISSIONS AND EVANGELISM

The agency to whom the Lord committed the winning of lost souls is the local church. It needs to have definite plans and programs concerning both evangelism and missions. The deacon should have a very particular interest in the plans for evangelism and the program of worldwide missions. A spirit of true evangelism among the deacons will serve to inspire the rest of the church in the great task of soul winning.

A. A Deacon's Personal Witness

Apart from any organized program of the church, each deacon should be a personal witness for Jesus Christ. The best witness of any Christian is not the planned program of witness in the church but his casual witness to all with whom he comes in contact. Whether on his job, traveling, shopping, or doing anything else that brings him in contact with people, the deacon should be alert to the opportunity to witness.

Every community has vast numbers of people who have never had the experience of conversion. Many of these will never be reached through planned programs. But the deacons of a church will have contact with many of these in their various relations throughout the community. Whenever they are brought together with these in any type of relationship, deacons should be alert to an opportunity to speak to the spiritual needs in their lives.

B. The Visitation Program

Each deacon should also be involved in the visitation program of the church. This visitation program should be separate and apart from the watchcare program mentioned in the previous chapter. That program had to do with church members. The church visitation program should be a systematic program of witness to the unchurched in the community.

The deacons should be alert to every means of discovering these prospects for witness. The names and addresses of visitors to the church should be ascertained by the deacons or ushers. Inherent in every church fellowship is another group of prospects—the relatives and friends of members. The deacons should see to it that the names of these are gathered for visitation possibilities. The deacons could lead in a program of door-to-door canvasing of the homes in the community. Whatever means of finding prospects is used, the deacons should be involved in the process.

When it comes to actual participation in visitation, the deacons should be leaders. Their example can be the great inspiration for other members of the church.

Though the deacons usually have many responsibilities, a significant part of their work should be concentrated upon the unsaved. Those outside the fellowship of the church and those who are unsaved should constantly burden the heart of the consecrated deacon. That burden should lead him out to win them to Christ.

The deacons should be the chief assistants to the pastor in the altar work of the church. Whether the persons who respond to the invitation of the pastor have been previously witnessed to by them or not, the deacons should meet them at the altar and aid them in making the decision which they came forward to make. Deacons who feel inadequate to do altar work should ask their pastor to train them in this vital service. The response to an invitation to join the church, to be saved, or to bring any problem before the Lord is an important decision in the life of an individual. Deacons should know how to interview the candidate in a loving, understanding way. They should know how to test the sincerity of the one responding and his desire to make a decision. Deacons need to be able to bring the person at the altar to an understanding of what all is involved in their decision. When situations arise that a deacon cannot handle, he should call the pastor to deal further with the person. By dealing properly with a mourner at the altar, the deacon may win his confidence and become that person's spiritual guide in succeeding days.

C. The Missions Program

Spreading the gospel at home or abroad is missions. The term has come to refer to evangelistic work away from the local church. Evangelism in our nation and bordering territories is generally referred to as "home missions" and that to lands abroad as "foreign missions." Accepting this terminology, the deacon should be a supporter of both home and foreign missions.

It will always be true that the pastor is the key to maintaining a world concept of Christian witness in the local church. However, deacons will be the channels through which he will project his outlook on missions. The deacons should reflect the pastor's concern for missions in all their activities.

Missions is much more than monthly gifts to missionaries. In fact, a program that only supplies money is a poor one. The missions program in a church should evolve out of a concern for the lost people around the globe. Deacons should have this burden for lost men wherever they are found. This burden should lead the church to prayer for lost men and for someone to go as witnesses. Out of each church that is burdened for lost souls around the world there should eventually come those who respond to carry the gospel. The deacons in conversation and official actions should always keep the burden for evangelizing the lost before the church. Out of this will grow financial support for missions. The deacons in their planning and recommendations should be generous in urging support for the cause of missions around the world. Anything less than a gospel for the whole world is inadequate. Deacons should be men of vision who can see the world lost, but Jesus as Savior for all.

Chapter Ten

STEWARDSHIP AND CHURCH FINANCE

A. A Personal Example
B. A Promotional Worker
C. The Distribution Of Funds

Conclusion

Chapter Ten

STEWARDSHIP AND CHURCH FINANCE

The full consecration of a Christian calls for him to yield what he *is* to Christ. Being a good steward calls for him to yield what he *has* to the Lord. Stewardship involves the responsibility of the believer to his Lord in regard to the things which have been entrusted to his care. Though this involves time, talent, and other things, it also includes our financial means. Stewardship to God in property is the material side of personal consecration to God. Every Christian is a steward but the deacon should be an example and leader to all the other members. The deacons by example and precept can provide a most effective challenge in the matter of stewardship.

A. A Personal Example

One of the chief concerns of the deacon will be the financial strength of the church. A church will never be any stronger than its adherence to the scriptural plan for the finance of the church. That plan outlined in the Scriptures for the support of God's work is found in tithes and offerings. The tithe is the starting point of every believer's stewardship. The tithe is the minimum for any member. To give less than the tithe is to rob God according to the Scriptures (Malachi 3:8). Along with the pastor, the deacons are the examples to the rest of the church in the stewardship of giving. Deacons who are covetous and keep back for themselves that which belongs to God are a bad example of proper stewardship. Salvation is received from the Lord without money and without a price. A dedicated deacon will find that his service is a costly thing in life and activity. He will immediately assume some of the tremendous responsibilities and costs by being a good steward.

The deacon, to fill his position effectively, must recognize the basis of all stewardship—that God is the owner of all material things and persons. As Paul wrote, " . . . ye are not your own? For ye are bought with a price . . . . " And as the psalmist said, "The earth is the LORD's, and the fulness thereof" (Psalm 24:1). Recognizing this, stewardship will become mandatory in a deacon's heart (Luke 14:26-33). By placing the demands of his Lord first in his life, the deacon will be a proper example to the rest of the church. A deacon who does not set an example in the distribution of his material benefits will probably not be followed in other areas of service.

Deacons who are specially blessed with financial assets have an increased responsibility in the matter of church finance. As previously stated, the tithe is the minimum. However, every believer is responsible for proper stewardship of the ninety percent as well. Accountability to God in the greater amounts is also a vital part of one's stewardship. A deacon with the ability to give must be foremost in the exercise of his possibilities.

B. A Promotional Worker

The deacon is a promotional worker in all aspects of stewardship and church finance. Not only does he set an example with his tithes and offerings, but he is a teacher and promoter of finance for all the enterprises of the church. As the pastor leads out in financial programs, the deacons can be leaders among the membership in seeing that goals are achieved. Their vocal support of the denominational plan of support, designated giving to missions and education, and any church expansion plans can ensure that the goals are reached.

The sin of covetousness prevails in churches as in the world. Church after church experiences the fact that only half of its membership gives anything to the support of the gospel causes. In many churches only about one-fourth of the church gives to the support of the work of Christ. The deacons by their teaching and challenge of the members can do much to cure this wrong; and, by doing so, increase the involvement of the church in support of the Lord's work.

Too many churches are hesitant to press the matter

of church finances. The pastor is often hesitant out of fear someone will think he is seeking a salary increase. The deacons, as laymen, can assume the brunt of financial campaigns in an effort to produce an adequate program of finance in the local church for all causes. Although giving will always be left up to the voluntary spirit of each believer, the deacons by their precept and practice can produce other givers who contribute systematically and joyfully to the work of the Lord. Giving is a part of spiritual living. Not giving is an evidence of spiritual problems. Each pastor should support his deacons as they lead the rest of the members in the worship and service of God through giving.

C. The Distribution of Funds

Our tithes and offerings should be given into the church treasury. The church as a whole decides through a budget or definite action how the money is spent. However, the board of deacons will always be a large influence on the distribution of the Lord's money. The deacons should recognize their great responsibility in this matter. They should never get a sense of proprietorship about the money in the treasury. It is not theirs. It belongs to the Lord. Through prayer they should seek under the leadership of the Holy Spirit to recommend distribution of the funds where it will do most to extend the Kingdom of Christ. Although one deacon may prefer strong support to one missionary or to one particular cause, he should try to see the need in all areas of the work. It is easy to get people to spend money on the local church. It is more difficult to get them to spend for outside causes. The board of deacons can be a big influence in balancing the spending between local needs and worldwide ministries. The deacons should be acquainted with all phases of the work in the denomination. This will enable them to explain the relationship of the local church to the larger areas of service. Through their knowledge they can challenge the church to give to the support of the causes on the state and national levels.

Conclusion

Deacons who read this may be astounded at what has been projected as the tasks of deacons. To do all that has been suggested would probably require that they go on salary as their pastor. What has been written has been recorded to reveal to deacons the enormity of their task. The possibilities for service and witness are unlimited.

The deacon is to be an involved man. He is not to hold the honor of his office with no accountability to service. In accepting the honor placed upon him he also accepted the burden of a ministry. His individual church may not require him to do all the things outlined in this book. However, every man who bears the title of a deacon should strive with God's help to become the servant of the church which he is supposed to be. By so doing deacons will " . . . purchase to themselves a good degree, and great boldness in the faith which is in Christ Jesus" (1 Timothy 3:13). That is their reward.